Dearest Abee,

Christmas 2011

I know you will love

when you sing this song, I know you feel
the spirit. Always remember that "Jesus
loves you". And we love you. Love,

Grammy
&
Grandpy

Gethsemane,
JESUS LOVES ME

Front Cover: *I Will Dry Your Tears* © Simon Dewey, courtesy Altus Fine Art. For print information, visit www.altusfineart.com or call 801-763-9788.

All songs except *He Is Risen*—Words & music written by Melanie Hoffman, ©2007 Melanie Hoffman & C T L Music (ASCAP). All Rights Reserved.

He Is Risen: Text—Cecil Frances Alexander; Music: Joachim Neander; additional text by Melanie Hoffman ©2007 Melanie Hoffman & C T L Music (ASCAP). All Rights Reserved.

Cover and interior designed by Christina Marcano
Cover design copyright © 2016 Covenant Communications, Inc.
Published by Covenant Communications, Inc.
American Fork, Utah

Songs are taken from the album *Stories of Jesus* ℗ 2007 by Deseret Book Company
Words & Music by Melanie Hoffman
Arranged by Roger Hoffman
Recorded and Mixed at Hoffman House Studios
All Songs © 2007 C T L Music ASCAP
All rights reserved

Printed in the United States
First Printing: February 2016

22 21 20 19 18 17 16   10 9 8 7 6 5 4 3 2

ISBN: 978-1-62108-519-5

Gethsemane,
JESUS LOVES ME

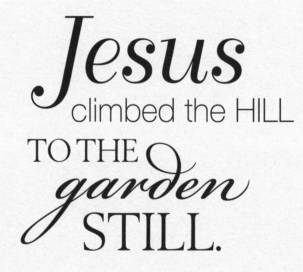

Jesus climbed the HILL TO THE *garden* STILL.

His *steps* were heavy AND SLOW.

Love
and a prayer
took Him there
TO THE PLACE
ONLY HE
COULD *go.*

Simon Dewey

GETHSEMANE.

Jesus loves me.

So He went *willingly* TO GETHSEMANE.

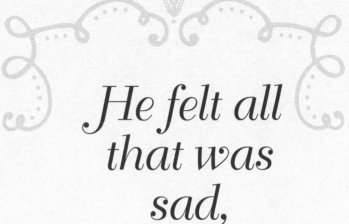

He felt all that was sad,

wicked or bad,

All the pain
we would ever
know.

WHILE HIS FRIENDS
WERE ASLEEP
He fought to keep
*His promise
made
long ago.*

15

GETHSEMANE.

Jesus loves me.

So He went
willingly
to
Gethsemane.

The *hardest* thing
that ever was done,

the

GREATEST
PAIN
that ever was known,

the
biggest battle
that ever was
WON,
THIS WAS DONE
BY
Jesus!

The fight was
WON
by *Jesus!*

GETHSEMANE.

Jesus loves me.

SO HE GAVE
HIS GIFT TO ME
IN
Gethsemane.

GETHSEMANE.

Jesus loves me.

SO
HE GIVES
His gift
to me
from
Gethsemane.

Gethsemane

Words & Music by
Melanie Hoffman
Arranged by
Roger Hoffman

Je - sus loves me.___ So He went will - ing - ly

B♭   E♭   A♭   B♭

To Geth - se - ma - ne. He felt all that was sad,

A♭   B♭   C min   C min   B♭

wick - ed or bad, All the pain we would ev - er know While His friends were a - sleep He

G min 7   A♭   B♭   A♭   C min   B♭

fought to keep His pro - mise made long a - go.

G min   A♭   B♭   C min

35

Geth - se - ma - ne. Je - sus loves me. So He

E♭   B♭   E♭   C min   B♭   E♭

cresc. poco a poco

went will - ing - ly To Geth-se-ma - ne. The hard - est thing that

A♭   E♭   B♭   A♭   B♭   C min   *mf* A♭   B♭

mf

e - ver was done, The great - est pain that e - ver was known, The big - gest batt - le that e - ver was won,

E♭   B♭   A♭   B♭   E♭   B♭   A♭   B♭   C min   B♭

rit.   a tempo

This was done by Je - sus! The fight was won by Je - sus! Geth - se - ma -

A♭   E♭   B♭   *f* A♭   E♭   B♭   *mp* C min

f   *mf*

ne.   Je -   sus   loves   me.   So He gave His gift to

E♭   A♭   B♭   E♭   A♭   E♭

me   In Geth - se - ma - ne.   Geth - se - ma - ne.

B♭   A♭   B♭   C_{sus}{}^{4} C_{min}   A♭   B♭   E♭

Je - sus loves me.   So He gives His gift   to me   From Geth - se - ma -

A♭   B♭   E♭   A♭   E♭   B♭   A♭   B♭

ne.

C_{sus}{}^{4}   C_{min}   A♭   B♭   C_{sus}{}^{4}   C

Christ's
GIFT TO ME

Gethsemane, *Jesus Loves Me* is a song about something that happened to Jesus in a special garden in the land where He grew up. But it isn't just about Jesus: it is about every one of us. And it is the most important thing that has ever happened in the history of the world.

Late one night, Jesus went to the Garden of Gethsemane, a grove of olive trees that was located on the side of a small mountain just outside Jerusalem. He asked three of his disciples to wait at the garden gate for Him, and then he went inside the garden and knelt in prayer among the olive trees.

Then He did the hardest thing that anyone has ever been asked to do. And He did it because of His great love for all of us.

The story of Gethsemane actually starts before the world was even created. While we were all still living with Heavenly Father, He explained His plan to all of us. He wanted each of us to come to earth so we could get a body and so we could have the chance to make decisions and covenants. An important part of His plan was that we would return to live with Him again after our time on earth was over.

When we heard Heavenly Father's plan, we were all so excited! In fact, we shouted for joy! We could hardly wait to come to earth, where we would be part of a family and where we would be able to experience the things Heavenly Father had in store for us.

But there was something important about Heavenly Father's plan: if we wanted to return and live with Him, we had to keep all of His commandments. That means we could not commit any sins. Heavenly Father knew each of us would sometimes make mistakes, so He had to figure out how to help us.

He decided to give us a Savior, a person who would pay for our sins if we would believe in Him and repent. That made it possible to return and live with our families and Heavenly Father forever. Before this world was ever created, Heavenly Father chose Jesus Christ to be our Savior.

Jesus's job was not an easy one. He promised to come to earth, show us the way to live, never commit a sin, and then pay the price for our sins. By doing that, He would give each of us the chance to return and live with Heavenly Father again, something we could not do on our own.

All the prophets who have ever lived told the people on earth that the Savior would save us from our sins. They told people that Heavenly Father would be Jesus's Father and that a young woman named Mary would be His mother.

Finally, Jesus was born in a manger in Bethlehem. Jesus grew up with His mother, Mary, and her husband, Joseph. They took care of Him just like all parents take care of their children.

But Jesus was different from all the other boys and girls who have lived on earth: He was perfect. He never broke any of God's commandments. That must have been very hard, because He was tempted to do bad things just like all of us are tempted. But He loved Heavenly Father and us so much that He kept all of Heavenly Father's commandments. That was important, because the person who would pay for all our sins had to be perfect.

After Jesus taught the people on earth how to return to live with Heavenly Father, it was time for Him to do the very hardest thing that any person would ever do. He told His disciples that it was time for Him to die. But before He could die, He needed to perform the Atonement, which was the way He would pay for all of our sins.

And that takes us back to Gethsemane.

"For unto you is born this day in the city of David a Saviour, which is Christ the Lord. . . .

"And suddenly there was with the angel a multitude of the heavenly host praising God, and saying,

"Glory to God in the highest, and on earth peace, good will toward men."

—LUKE 2:11–14

Jesus knew that what He was about to do would hurt more than anything could ever hurt. As He prayed in Gethsemane, He fell on His face and asked Heavenly Father if there was *any* other way to do what He needed to do. But He also promised Heavenly Father that He would go ahead with the plan (see Matthew 26:39) because of His love for Heavenly Father and for us.

There in Gethsemane, Jesus paid the price for our sins. When we do something wrong, we feel so sorry. Jesus felt all the sadness that came with all the sins that everyone on earth would ever commit. His pain was so great that He bled from every pore of His skin. That kind of pain would have killed all of us; the only reason He could do it was because He was a god, since Heavenly Father was His father.

But He did more than just suffer for our sins. There in the garden, He suffered for all the hurt, grief, sadness, sickness, and pain we would ever have. Because He did that, He knows exactly how we feel in every situation, and He is ready to help us and comfort us, no matter what we are going through. It

41

Simon Dewey

was the hardest thing anyone has ever done and the greatest gift anyone has ever offered.

When He was finished with His prayer, Jesus was arrested, tied up, beaten with whips, made fun of, and spit on. Then the soldiers nailed Him to a cross and pounded the cross into the ground. Called *crucifixion,* it was the most painful way to kill someone, and Jesus was already weak from what had happened in Gethsemane. The soldiers left Him there on the cross to die.

Because Jesus was a god, He didn't have to die; no one could have killed Him. Clear up until the last minute, He could have changed His mind and decided to live. But He didn't. He wanted to finish Heavenly Father's plan because He loved Heavenly Father so much. But that's not all: He loved every one of us so much that He wanted to make it possible for us to return and live with Heavenly Father. He knew us all before He came to earth, and He loved every one of us with a love that we can't ever fully understand.

"Greater love hath no man than this, that a man lay down his life for his friends."

—John 13:15

And so that Friday night Jesus died; His spirit left His body. A kind man offered a tomb where Jesus's body could be placed, and His friends wrapped His body in clean cloth and placed it in the tomb. A huge stone was rolled in front of the tomb door to seal Jesus inside.

On Sunday when some women came to put some nice-smelling oil on the cloth around Jesus's body, they saw that the stone had been rolled away. The tomb was empty. He had risen, as He said He would do! He was the first person ever to die and then take up His body again! He had been *resurrected.* That was also part of Heavenly Father's plan. Because of the Atonement of Jesus Christ, everyone who ever lives—even those who do not obey any of the commandments—will be resurrected. It is a gift Jesus gave to everyone because of His great love. What Jesus did guarantees that we will all have our bodies when we return to live with Heavenly Father.

What Jesus did in Gethsemane was for us. It gives us hope. It gives us comfort. It means that whatever happens in our life, we can turn to Him for help. It means we will never, ever be left alone. It means that He is our very best friend, and He always will be. All of it is because of Gethsemane—and because Jesus loves us, every single one of us.

Art Credits

Light of the World © Howard Lyon Fine Art. For print information, visit www.howardlyon.com.

Walk With Me © Greg K Olsen. By arrangement with Greg Olsen Art, Inc. For more information about art prints by Greg Olsen, please visit www.GregOlsen.com or call 1-800-352-0107.

O My Father © Simon Dewey, courtesy Altus Fine Art. For print information, visit www.altusfineart.com or call 801-763-9788.

Hold On Tight © Liz Lemon Swindle. Courtesy of Foundation Arts. For print information, visit www.foundationarts.com.

The Master's Touch © Greg K Olsen. By arrangement with Greg Olsen Art, Inc. For more information about art prints by Greg Olsen, please visit www.GregOlsen.com or call 1-800-352-0107.

Go In Peace © Del Parson; for print information, visit www.delparson.com.

I Will Dry Your Tears © Simon Dewey, courtesy Altus Fine Art. For print information, visit www.altusfineart.com or call 801-763-9788.

Gethsemane © Howard Lyon Fine Art. For print information, visit www.howardlyon.com.

Let the Children Come © Liz Lemon Swindle. Courtesy of Foundation Arts. For print information, visit www.foundationarts.com.

Under His Wing © Jay Bryant Ward. Courtesy of Jay Bryant Ward Studios, LLC. For print information, visit JayBryantWard.com.

An Angel Strengthened Him © Del Parson; for print information, visit www.delparson.com.

Behold My Hands © Jeff Ward, courtesy Altus Fine Art. For print information, visit www.altusfineart.com or call 801-763-9788.

Mary Magdalene © Del Parson; for print information, visit www.delparson.com.

Lost and Found © Greg K Olsen. By arrangement with Greg Olsen Art, Inc. For more information about art prints by Greg Olsen, please visit www.GregOlsen.com or call 1-800-352-0107.

Encircled in His Love © Annie Henrie Nader, www. anniehenrie.com.

No Shoes © Del Parson; for print information, visit www.delparson.com.

He Lives © Simon Dewey, courtesy Altus Fine Art. For print information, visit www.altusfineart.com or call 801-763-9788.

Light In The Darkness © Dan Wilson. For print information, visit www.danwilsonportraits.com or call 801-787-0654.

Heavenward © Jeff Ward, courtesy Altus Fine Art. For print information, visit www.altusfineart.com or call 801-763-9788.

The Dawning of a New Day © Simon Dewey, courtesy Altus Fine Art. For print information, visit www.altusfineart.com or call 801-763-9788.